FALLEN

WAR IN WRITING

To commemorate
The start of the First World War 100 years ago.

References are also made to the Second World War
and other conflicts involving the UK

Compiled and edited by
Ishbel Kargar, Jean Gidman
and Tricia Statter.

Front cover by Tricia Statter

ORMSKIRK WRITERS
(Ormskirk Writers and Literary Society)
Est. 1963

Published by © OWL Publishing

British Library Cataloguing in Publication Data,
A Catalogue record for this book is available from the Britsh Library.
ISBN 978-1-873553-04-6

All rights reserved. No part of this book may be reproduced or transmitted in any form or by any means, electronic or mechanical including photocopying, recording or by any information storage and retrieval system, without permission from the publishers in writing.

Printed by Flexipress, Windmill Avenue, Ormskirk L39 4QB. Tel: 01695 576839.

All profits will be donated to Help For Heroes.

DEDICATION

We who live
beyond the times of many wars and tribulations,
hope to comfort and amuse those of us
who are left in sadness.

Remembering the precious ones we had to lose.

We who live as members of OWLS
present this book in tribute
to those whom you and we have known and lost.

Not dead but living in our memories.

We hear and see them as they were in life.

Cecil Beach

CONTENTS

Part One – Letters from the Front

Page	Title	Author
1	2nd Lt. Henry Corner Reynard	Richard Houghton
3	Guardsman Ralph Haddon Hill	Richard Houghton
6	Pte. Richard A. Halton	Richard Houghton
9	Pte. Robert Winrow	Joan Morris
11	Pte. William Martland	Richard Houghton
12	Sgt. Maj. Harold Keatley	Richard Houghton
13	Sgt. William Roberts	Patricia Ireland

Part Two – Poems

Page	Title	Author
19	November Remembers	Judy Ingman
20	Memorial	Cecil Beach
22	Rear Gunner	Tom McDonald
24	Offices of Love	Cecil Beach
25	Rachel's House	Patricia P. Jones
26	They think it's All Over	Tom McDonald
28	My great Uncle Burt	Tom McDonald
31	Politically Correct	Cecil Beach
32	A Soldier of the Great War	Tricia Statter

Part Three – Memoirs and Stories

Page	Title	Author
36	Waking the Lion	Cecil Beach
39	Dear Papa	Graham Walker
41	Missing Presumed Dead	Judy Ingman
47	The Love	Cecil Beach
45	Near Misses	Ishbel Kargar
49	Recollections of WW2	Jennifer Waite
51	The Home Front	Jean Gidman
53	Rocking The Rafters	Valerie Roche
59	The Kaiser in the Lake District	Ron Black
61	A Study in War	Keith Venables
64	Evacuees	Ishbel Kargar
66	Family Memories	Lynn Lawton
69	Edwin' Story	Patrick Waite
71	Women at War	Keith Venables
74	Murphy the Donkey	Tricia Statter

Part 1

Letters from the Front

The following letters appear as written, spelling and punctuation not edited.

2ND LIEUT. HENRY CORNER REYNARD,
D company, 1st Battalion, North Staffs Regiment. (ex Artists Rifles)
Killed in Action 25th Sept.1915, Loos.
(Listed on Loos Memorial)

Henry Reynard as a young boy with his mother and sister

2.10.1915
Telegram OHMS from Secretary, War Office
To: Mrs R. Reynard, Holly Bank, West Ewell, Epsom
2nd Lt H.C.Reynard S.Staffs Regt was reported missing 25/27 Sept
This does not necessarily mean that he was killed or wounded.

5.10.1915
Telegram OHMS from Secretary, War Office
To: Mrs Reynard, Holly Bank, W. Ewell, Epsom
2nd Lt H.C. Reynard S. Stafford Regt. Previously reported missing 25/27 now reported wounded.

7 Oct. 1915
Letter to: Casualty Dept. (Officer)
From: Holly Bank, West Ewell

Dear Sir,
Will you kindly give me any information, as to where 2nd Lieut. H.C.Reynard, D.Company 1st South Staffordshire Regt. is, and as to the nature of his wounds.
Yours faithfully,
R. Reynard (Mother)

19 Oct 1915
Note from Holly Bank, West Ewell - Rec'd War Office 20.10.1915
Mrs Reynard received a telegram Oct 2nd saying her son 2nd Lieut. H.C. Reynard 1st S. Staffs Regt was missing.
On Oct 5th she received another telegram saying that he was wounded not missing. She has been anxiously waiting each day for further news, and would feel very grateful if you can give any information as where he is, and as to the nature of his wounds, if serious.

30.10.1915
Telegram from Secretary, War Office to: Mrs R. Reynard, Holly Bank, West Ewell, Epsom
Deeply regret to inform you 2nd Lieut. H.C. Reynard S. Stafford Regt previously reported missing & wounded was Killed in Action 25th Sept. Lord Kitchener expresses his sympathy.

East Surreys, France. Reynard S. Lt. H.C. W&M Sept. 25 1915

He was my platoon officer – XIV
I saw him shot through both knees on the parapet of the German first line trenches. He was unable to move. We went on and he was left behind. We did not retire back and the ground on which we left him is still in our possession. We have never heard of him since.

Ref. L/Cpl. Egginton, 9304, D. Lewis Gun School, Etaples,
6th August 1916

GUARDSMAN RALPH HADDON HILL NO. 3
3rd Company, 3rd Battalion, Coldstream Guards.

Killed in Action 11/11/1917
No Grave but is on the Tyne Cot Memorial

Saturday Night Tattoo. 21.7.17

Dear Father,
I now take the pleasure in writing these few lines in reply to your letter which I received two days ago hoping this finds you all in the best of health as it leaves me at present A1
Glad to hear you have got Sid off in joining the Army, and if he takes his brothers advice he will never join unless he is forced to.
Yes father I never released how good of a father and mother I had till I enlisted in the Army and I know I will be a different son & brother to you all when I return home that's if God spares me which I hope he will because Fritz has not got a bullet or a shell with my name on and we will all be returning this year. I think I have heard that he is bobbing on Peace just now, hoping it is true.
Dad I am sorry I said that about me going to the Pits when I returned but I did not like the Army at the time and I said to myself if I had been at the Pits I would not have been here but if I had not enlisted I would not worth been called a son to you because I was being led away and not seeing it

although I know it and we all have Mr ? to thank for me seeing it and so I enlisted to get in the right road. And we will have a happy home when I come home.

Sorry to hear Dad that you are getting poor crops this year. I wish I was with you all that Sunday night when you wrote that letter down at the flats. I have got them pictures at night when I lay down to sleep, the walks we enjoy when we all use to go out which will come again. It is of no use Cousin Mary bobbing over her lad coming home because he is a fool when he writes & tells his people he is coming home because it is best to wait when you are landed in Blighty and then wire then you are sure of getting home.

We are having hot weather here now but it is alright for when you are at rest and lines but rotten for marching with but we must not complain because we have not had much marching lately.

Well Dear Dad and Ma I hardly know what to write so I will draw to a close so Goodnight and May God Bless and Watch over you all till I return.

From Your Loving Son

Ralph

Xxxxx

Will write 2 days time

Nov. 23rd 1917   B.E.F.

Dear Sir,

This is the 3rd letter I have written to you notifying you of parcels safely received. As your latest parcel was dated Sept 21st it would appear my letters have not been reaching you. It would also appear that you have not yet been notified of the Death in Action of your brother M.742 Pt Hill on the 11th inst. The contents of parcels received have been issued to his comrades as stated in my previous letters to you. I am so sorry if my letters have gone astray, & forgive me for telling you of your brother's death in such an abrupt way, but you certainly should have been notified of your brother's death officially before now. Trusting you have received my previous 2 letters & that the procedure with regards to the contents of parcels will meet with your approval.

Believe Me

Yours Truly

Charles F. Dow (Coy Sgt Major)

Withy Spring Cottage
Farnham Common
Nr. Slough,
Bucks
4th Jan 1918

Dear Mrs Hill,
I have only just heard of your son Ralph's Death & felt I must write & tell you how sorry I am.
I knew him, about three months before he left Windsor. Did you hear if he was wounded first. The report I had said "Killed in Action Nov. 11th". The last letter I had was dated Sept 3rd so I have been wondering what happened, as it was so unlike him not to write.
He volunteered for that draft otherwise he might have been here several months longer. I was with him the night before he left here & saw him off the next morning May 24th & seemed very jolly & said he left all to the one above, who he knew would bring him through safely.
How terrible it all seems. I have just lost my only Brother of twenty.
Poor Boys I don't suppose they were sorry to go from the horrors of this wicked war, no one knows what they must have suffered, but there is relief now to know that they are at rest after nobly doing their bit.
I will now conclude hoping you will forgive the liberty I have taken in writing to you & accept my deepest sympathy.
Yours sincerely,
Ethel A Pusey.

PRIVATE RICHARD A. HALTON

From the Ormskirk Advertiser 24 December 1914

LETTERS FROM THE FRONT
A BURSCOUGH MAN'S CONFIDENCE

The following is a copy of a letter received by Mr James Halton, School Lane, Burscough Bridge from his son, Private R. A. Halton, who is now serving with the Liverpool Scottish:

December 11 1914

"We have today returned to billet after another three days in the trenches and I am glad to say that we have again been exceedingly fortunate, although we have had to leave one or two of the fellows behind. Barker and Curtis are still alright, and so are Newton and Walker.

I feel more confident each time we go up as the officers and men are such a cool crowd, and get on extremely well. In fact, the regulars themselves admit they are a "cool lot," and they are very much struck with the conduct of the battalion in the field, which they state, exceeds their expectations.

We are attached to what is supposed to be a crack brigade. By the way, those "Jack Johnson's" don't half make a mess. You could drive a horse in to the hole they make. We have, however, had very little reason to fear these things, as they are mostly used against our heavy artillery.

We were inspected by the King the other day. I should think he must have a pretty busy time inspecting the troops over here. You would be surprised if you were to go to the trenches, and see the animals such as pigs and goats running about. If you desire to send anything, please forward chocolate or sweets instead of cigarettes or tobacco, as we now get as much as we can get through".

AMONGST THE "JACK JOHNSONS"

Private R. A. Halton (Burscough), of "The Liverpool Scottish" in a further letter to his parents under date 17th December, writes:-

"We have just returned from the trenches again, and are now enjoying a rest. We have now had nine days in action altogether, and am glad to say that our casualties have been exceptionally light. So far, I think, our total losses have been one officer and three men killed, and about twenty wounded.

Things had been fairly quiet up to last Saturday, when a big action began. It opened on Monday morning with a terrific artillery bombardment. A tremendous number of guns were engaged, and at night the scene was splendid, the flashes of the guns making a splendid spectacle. All kinds and sizes were represented, from the ordinary field gun to the heaviest siege gun. The enemy were in a wood, and seemed likely to stick there. After the artillery had given them a pretty warm time, our infantry attacked their trenches.

The fighting continued all day, and at night we were sent up again in support. By the way we were up on Saturday for the third time in place of one of the infantry battalions, who were to make the attack on Monday, and on Monday morning we left the trenches and went behind in other words, stood in support, and moved up again after the attack, and came out for our usual rest last night. Our chaps are getting a jolly good name from the "Tommies" who are very much struck by their coolness under fire. In some places our trenches are within thirty yards of the Germans, so that you will see it is really marvellous that the casualty list is so light.

We had a rather exciting experience the other night taking up ammunition to the firing line. We had to carry it in boxes for about a mile to the trenches across fields, in which there are a great many "Jack Johnson" holes, and barbed wire entanglements and trenches. The night was very dark, and there was about a foot of mud on the fields, which made it very difficult to walk. The boxes are carried by two men, one hold of each handle, and if one chap happened to pull a bit to one side, the other slipped and fell. Well, after falling into two or three holes and slipping in the mud, we got to within 30 yards of the German "firelight". These things can be seen for miles and light up the whole country. When the thing went off we were all together, we fell down flat, and lay still till it died out.

However, we got the ammunition up all right without any of the party being hit, and were just getting along on the top of the trench, when up went another light. We all fell flat and waited. One or two shots were fired, but we got through safely again. It was very funny, however, to see all the chaps down on their knees with their heads down in the mud.

I am in the best of spirits. The weather is a lot better than it was, and not very cold just now."

Following promotions, he became Captain Richard Halton, South Lancashire Regiment. 1917-1918

N.B. A "Jack Johnson' was the nickname given by the British to describe the impact of the heavy black German 15cm artillery shell. Jack Johnson was a boxer famous for his powerful punch.

PRIVATE ROBERT WINROW

Copy of pencil written letter

55800 5th Platoon,
B Company 1st R.W.F.
France
H.Q.
25/1/17

Dear Mother,

Just a few lines to let you know I received the parcels alright. The mince pie was. A.1. I ate it all at one meal. I was thinking of asking you to send me a flash light, it is the handiest thing you could send. Well we have moved to another village for six weeks training. I am having it quite easy now, just running an order now and again. We are having some very cold weather here at present, freezing very hard, but it is better than wet weather.

I wonder how James is going on, if he is in the trenches he will be nearly frozen to death. I was lucky to drop on him so soon. I had about 3 miles to walk to see him, but if it had been 10 miles I should have gone.

I am sleeping in a barn, plenty of straw and blankets. We are quite warm at night.

I got a parcel from F. Gale. It was fags. I wrote back and thanked him for them.

Well Mother I am in the pink of health, hoping you and all at home are the same. I am glad that our Jack is sticking the course in England and I hope he never comes out here, there is enough of us out here, but I don't think it will last long now, I think we have them beat. I suppose J. Smallshaw wont like the idea of coming out here again, he knows what it is like here.

Well I have nothing more to say this time,
        from your loving son Bob

Private Robert Winrow, my mother's youngest brother, son of Richard and Elizabeth Winrow, Rope Makers from Derby Street, Ormskirk, joined the Kings Liverpool Regiment but was transferred to the Welsh Fusiliers.

He had been employed as a plumber at T. Balls, Derby Street.

He was killed 4th May 1917 aged 24 in the Battle of Arras at Bullecourt. He has no grave but his name is on the Arras Memorial in Faubourg-Damiens Cemetery, Arras.

His brothers, James and Jack, also served in France and returned home severely injured.

Contributed by Joan Morris

PRIVATE WILLIAM MARTLAND No 64959

Pencil Letter on Y.M.C.A headed paper.
Company C 5 Rom King's Liverpool,
Llannion Barracks
Pembroke Dock, S Wales
Tuesday 2/3/1917

Dear Uncle and Ant,
Just a few lines to you hoping to find you in good health as it leaves me at present and I got your letter on Friday night and if you did not get one of the photo I sent you must write back and let me no and I will got some more and send one and you muist send back how John Figles Ralph went on and I send my best wishes to all and now I close my letter with good Luck and good night.
From William Martland
Llanion Barracks

William Martland of Stanley Street ,Burscough, No. 66813 32/ Royal Fusiliers was killed in Action 7/8/1917 aged 20.

He has no grave but is listed on the Menin Gate.

REGIMENTAL SERGEANT MAJOR HAROLD KEATLEY, MC.
Green Howards/ Yorkshire Regiment

Killed in action 7th April 1917 at the battle of Arras.
He is listed on the Arras Memorial.

27.2.17

Dear Sergeant Major,

Thanks for your letter of the 15th.
I am pleased to tell you that you have been given the Military Cross for your part in our little attack of the 8th. There's no doubt you deserved it and I heartily congratulate you, as do all the rest of us. LCpl. Marsden has the D.C.M.; LCpl. Stevenson the M.M; and I myself am the luckiest of all, for I have got the D.S.O. and a month's leave thrown in! I think I am the luckiest man in the battalion.

I am sorry to say Mr. Griffiths, Mr. Collet & Mr. Lolly have all died of wounds in Hospital. Sergt. Wrightson has died too.

I hope you are enjoying the course better now than you did at first and that the work isn't quite as strenuous. I certainly thought I was doing you a good turn in putting you down for it and I hope it will turn out so! At any rate you will be able to show off when you come back full of the latest drill and with your blue and white ribbon up.
Best wishes & congratulations.

Yours sincerely,
W. D. Wilkinson.

SERGEANT WILLIAM ROBERTS

12th King's Liverpool Regiment, 20th Light Division, Army Number 148370

My paternal grandfather, William Roberts, was born on the 22nd June, 1891, at 57 High Street, Skelmersdale, the son of Joseph Roberts, a coalminer, and his wife Harriet. William grew up and in due course himself became a coalminer at a local pit. He was a physically fit young man, 6ft. 5 inches tall, and a keen footballer.

In January 1913, aged 22, William married a local girl, Catherine Heath, and they had two sons, Thomas born 1913 and William born early 1915.

In September 1914, William volunteered for action in World War 1, enlisting with coalminer friends from Skelmersdale. They were all patriotic young men, looking for adventure and sharing the common belief that the war would be over by Christmas.

William enlisted and served with the 12th King's Liverpool Regiment, 20th Light Division, while his brother, Joseph, enlisted in the East Lancashire Regiment. William saw continual action throughout the First World War with his regiment, the enclosed photo with his wife and sons being taken at a studio during a brief leave in late 1915 or early 1916.

William was soon promoted to Sergeant. His Division served on the Western Front for the whole of the war, taking part in many of the significant actions.

In 1916 the Battle of Mount Sorrel, a local operation in which the Division recaptured the height with the Canadians; the Battle of Delville Wood*; the Battle of Guillemont* ; the Battle of Flers-Courcelette*; the Battle of Morval* and the Battle of Le Transloy*.

Then in 1917, William's Division was involved in forcing the German retreat to the Hindenburg Line; the Battle of Langemarck**; the Battle of the Menin Road Ridge** and the Battle of Polygon Wood** Then finally that year, the Cambrai Operations.

In 1918, William and his colleagues fought at the Battle of St Quentin***, the actions at the Somme crossings***, and the Battle of Rosieres***. His Division was withdrawn after the heavy fighting of the Somme battles, moving in April 1918 to an area south west of Amiens. During the summer months it received new drafts of men and was later involved at the Battle of the Selle****^; the Battle of Valenciennes****; the Battle of the Sambre**** and the passage of the Grand Honelle.

William's Division was in the area between Bavay and Maubeuge when the Armistice came into effect at 11am, 11th November, 1918. In all the 20th (Light) Division had suffered the loss of 35,470 killed, wounded and missing.

William distinguished himself in action; he received the Military Medal and Bar for gallantry during the Battles of the Somme and the Battle of Ypres, which included his going back out under heavy fire to carry the badly injured to safety. He was also mentioned in Despatches.

He survived the war, as did his brother Joseph Roberts (who had been taken prisoner of war), but of his coalminer friends who had volunteered with him in 1914, William was one of only two to return, the other being badly injured.

However, at the end of the war, William came home to find himself a young widower and his two small sons motherless, his wife having tragically died of pneumonia in early 1918. His sons were initially looked after by her relatives in Skelmersdale, while William himself sought work with the Liverpool Police, where he stayed for the rest of his working life, rising to the rank of Sergeant. He remarried in 1920 to a war widow, May Allen, and they lived in Anfield for many years. (William's elder son, Thomas, born 1913, was taken to live with his father's new family in Anfield, while his younger brother, William junior, born 1915, remained in Skelmersdale with his aunt, Emma Abrams and family).

William and his second wife, May, had two children together, Norman and Marjorie, born in the 1920s. In their retirement, William and May moved to the Mold area in North Wales, where William died in 1958.

Patricia Ireland

2nd June 2014

*   Phases of the Battles of the Somme, 1916

**   Phases of the Third Battles of Ypres

***   Phases of the First Battles of the Somme, 1918

**** Phases of the Final Advance in Picardy

Part 2

POETRY

NOVEMBER REMEMBERS

Remember, November remembers,
Remembers, all those who died.
Eleventh month, eleventh day, eleventh hour
Every family member, who cried, who died.
November remembers and minds.
Blood red poppies worn to remind
The deaths of those who gave their lives.
White poppies born, dove white to release
Love and hope for future peace.

What peace does November remember?
Fourteen-eighteen war to end all wars,
Followed by world war two, in aftermath
Vietnam, Falklands, and again Iraq,
Afghanistan, and where next we ask?

November, every year remembers and tries
Eleventh month, eleventh day, eleventh hour
Dong, Dong, never ending November long, longs
To remind the end to wars, dong, dong
Peace floating feathers on the wings of the dove,
Bloodied red by countries' battle songs.
Families' grievings across the ages
November always remembers, but nothing changes.

Judy Ingman

MEMORIAL

He died, that soldier standing there, with rifle by his puttee'd legs.
Upon the marble plinth. Up there above the homeless youth, who begs
Below the counting house, where tall computer banks of memory block
Sift, calculating shares of all, and deal in shifting gilts and stock.

While rich men with precocious greed
Seek more and pass the homeless ones in need,
Below that noble soldier's brow.

Is that a tear upon his eye,
And is he asking mutely now, "Was it for this I had to die?
In Faulklands? And in Normandy? And Flanders, where to end all wars
I died, so children could be free here, in this pleasant land of yours.

Care for these children, they are mine and yours, as me, returned to you;
Born of our heritage and line. Give them that which to me was due.

I was the child you cast aside. I was the sacrifice. I paid.
I was your conscience, I who died. I was the error that you made.
I was your future, I your youth. I am the child you raised and bore.
I am your edifice to truth. I am your hopes. I am no more."

C E Beach 1989

Picture sent in by June Beach.

REARGUNNER

    During our basic training in the National Service days, we had a very young, inhibited Medical Officer, whose duty it was to instruct us rookies on the hazards of army life. He was always giving us lectures on safety. One thing I can still remember him saying on every occasion, (and he'd say it with some reservation) was that: "It makes you go deaf;" and "you should always use protection;" but in his naivety, he never told us what *it* was that made us go deaf. On the last days of our basic training we were introduced to the 25 pounders on the firing range. It was only then that I thought I realized what the M.O meant by protection, the noise was unbearable. So I hastily equipped myself with a pair of ear-muffs.
    This poem is about a mate of mine called Jeff, who didn't bother to use any sort of protection.

Tom McDonald

When Jeff was a gunner,
In the Royal Armoured Corps,
He fired large guns on the range,
But he near dun a runner,
When his ears got sore,
So they let him drive jeeps for a change.

This gave him more leeway to go out on the town,
And to be with the girls of that city,
They were girls of renown,
Dressed up in silk gown,
But their faces were not very pretty.

They used too-much make-up and bleached their long hair,
And they increased their height with high–heels,
They'd slink along sidewalks, sometimes as a pair,
And spend lots of time doing deals.

Then Jeff's hearing got worse,
So he approached the M.O. who said he should have known better.
He said, "Make an appointment with Stephanie, my nurse,
And she'll give you a clinical letter.

Then go to the clinic, where you must take the tests,
And they'll tell of original sin,
About dolly-bird-chicks, who will feather their nests,
And young gunners who are soon taken in."

The clinic was crowded with Gunners like Jeff,
And they suffered a similar complaint,
It was called 'Gunners Ear,
So it would appear,
But the diagnosis he heard was too faint.

He went back to Steph...
He said "I'm still a bit deaf,"
She said, "It's because you have an infection,
You've been over-active,
In matters attractive,
And you haven't been using protection"...

He said. "How do you know?"
She said, "Ask the M.O.
Just tell him you were sent there by Steph."
He said "I've told him before,
When I fired the twelve bore,
It's the banging that makes me go deaf."

She said: "On that we agree,
But what's worrying me,
Is you do nothing to allay all our fears,"
"Don't worry" said he,
"From this packet of three,
I'll take two to stuff in my ears."

"Oh Jeff!" said Steph,
"You should know why you're deaf,
It's because of the company you keep.
It's not the noise from the gun,
It's you boys having fun,
So take care when you're parking your jeep."

He finally saw sense,
Saying "I must have been dense,
But you deserve my most heartfelt of thanks."
She said "Go back to your Corps,
There's talk of a war,
But let's hope that you're not firing blanks."

OFFICES OF LOVE

I take you back, about the start of world war two
When everybody had an outside loo
And smoky fires, when winter nights were cold
When I was just about fourteen years old.

Early morning I would hear
My father going down the stairs,
Fill the kettle, light the gas
And rake the ashes from the grate.
I'd sit up in my bed beside
The Jack Frost painted window, then

Pull on my school shirt over head
With vest inside, and put my foot on the lino that
Was cold, and cramp would make me dance
Before I followed down to find the fire
Coaxed with a shovel or the news,
Or to the pegged rug shooting sparks,

While father shaved and cooked fried bread
With ripe tomatoes, bacon, eggs
To be my breakfast. With his legs
Dressed in his old ex-army pants.
He'd take my mother tea in bed,
Then get his old bike from the shed and ride to work.

The simple offices of love
That he performed I well recall,
Reminding me, that all above
The greatest things we do are small.

C.E.Beach

RACHEL'S HOUSE

A farm stood at the end of the road
Charlie collected milk in a jug
Running, spilling, juggling
Boy dreams cradled warmly in haylofts
Through cobbled yard and much strewn midden
Splashed with ducks and noisy with crowing.

He returned to the neat house with bay windows
Displayed the jug in the tiny kitchen on the sill
A canopy of bedfellow, bread loaves, bay leaves
Jams, tall glass tinkling jars
Heralded the ascent of other culinary herbs
Bursting energies, like perfumery bubbles
Dissipate to ceilings, recline in spaces
In Rachel's house.

Below stairs in the darkened pantry
With shelves crammed tight
Pickled plums for Sunday lunch
To be stewed, pulped, for soft sweet palates
Forks, spoons, clatter from green lined drawers
Regimented on crisp clean cloth, busy with crumbs
Scooped diligently with brush to narrow waiting tray.

Shuffling chairs, voices mingle
Newspaper headings of distant wars
Rumbling guns, parcels in brown paper
Charlie's letter, Rachel clutched with care
And donging dutifully the old clock chimes
Settles, an autonomy, challenging, brooding
It is late, history moves on
Moments fragment, lose potency
Are gone.

Patricia P. Jones

THEY THINK IT'S ALL OVER. (*A vague history of the 20th Century.*)

When The Keizer first started the war,
He thought he would give us what for,
Near the end of his mission,
He had no ammunition,
So the Irish Free State gave him more.

"We've got enough guns", he said without smile,
"But no whiz bombs to shoot down our foes."
So they sent a stockpile, of this lethal missile,
And that's when the problem arose,

All of his guns started jammin',
'cos the ammo' they sent was all duds,
It created a great Irish famine,
'Cos they'd mixed up their bombs with their spuds.

This caused the Keizer to panic,
As his battle went right off the boil,
So Shamus an Irish mechanic,
Said: "Dunk all your taters in oil."

He said: "Get all your ammo and dip it in this,
And aim at whoever you choose,
Just hold your breath and pray you don't miss,
This time your guns won't refuse".

When the battle commenced the very next day,
His armies were licking their lips
For their guns became tired,
As each one backfired,
And they found themselves covered in chips.
(*Is that why they bombed our chippy?*)

The battle was won 'cos their guns were all broke,
And we won every battle thereafter,
For we tannoyed the joke, about that Shamus bloke,
So each wave of attack died of laughter.

In the next war Adolf Hitler would try,
And we said he was mad, who can blame us,
And not one of our soldiers could understand why
Like the Keizer he still trusted that Shamus

He said: "Let's point the guns at every last Jew,
To show that I'm no ignoramus,"
But to the Jewish, deep fry
'Twas like cash from the sky
And Cohen's crisps have since become famous.

But just think, if Hitler, - had won the war,
He'd have changed this old England's regime,
We'd have no Churchill to jaw, jaw-jaw,
Instead of that, a nightmare dream.

And if you ever came to England, my lad,
Sometime in the future or later,
Would you have thought of our regent
As a spud that's gone bad?
Or the acolyte ruler, King Edward potater.

Tom McDonald.

My Great Uncle Burt

I had a great uncle who fought in the First World War, Teddy Jenkins. I don't know what he did in the war, but when I was a kid his name always cropped up in conversation, between the older members of my family and always with warm affection, and there was always lots of laughter when his name was mentioned. We kids never really listened to adults talking in large gatherings, but when we were playing cowboys or cops and robbers, we'd heard enough to make all my cousins and me argue, as to who was going to be Teddy Jenkins, in whatever game we were playing, usually at my Grannie's house.

When I was older I got to wondering about my great Uncle Joey, and I thought I'd ask my Mum and Dad about him. One day when I happened to mention his name they were all ears, as I said. "Hey, do you remember Teddy Jenkins who fought in the Great War?" and my dad said: "Yes, what would you like to know about him?" I said, (wanting to know if he was dad's relation or mum's), "Well whose side was he actually on?" Indignantly they both said in unison, "He was on our side!"

And because I never found out exactly what he did that kept him in my family's thoughts, I used my imagination.

But I've changed the name of my Great Uncle Teddy to Great Uncle Burt, to protect the innocent.

Tom McDonald

Schnel Shock.

According to history and my great Uncle Burt,
Who fought in the First Great World War,
It was an unfathomed mystery why he should desert,
Being loyal as he was, to his Royal Armoured Corp.

It was said at his trial he'd been over the wall,
To fraternise with Fritz from the Boche,
But he'd only answered a brief nature call,
In private, because he was posh.

The lawyer for defence spoke out in his favour,
And ignorance was the name of the plea,
But there was no recompense, for absent behaviour,
Though he'd only gone out for a riddle-me-ree,

And while he was standing just outside his trench,
When he'd only been gone for two shakes,
A German called Fritz, was admiring his bits,
And this gave my uncle the Quakes.

So my traumatised uncle broke out in a run,
He was trembling like he'd seen a ghost,
After saying politely, 'no thanks', to the Hun,
He stood guard once again at his post,

He was still shaking when they came to relieve him,
And they said it was a sign he was scared,
About Fritz, they wouldn't believe him,
The excuse was the worst that they'd heard.

The Court Martial declared that my uncle,
Was someone who should be forgot,
For "the Regiment don't need this carbuncle",
So next morning at dawn would be shot.

Then a Captain named Bligh woke him up,
Not the one from the 'Bounty,' not him,
This one was a soldier and he grabbed uncle's shoulder,
Saying: "This blindfold's for you, Sonny Jim".

Then Padre informed, my great uncle Burt
One request, he would be allowed,
To stop blood from spilling and spoiling his shirt
Which could be used later, in place of a shroud.

The firing squad lined up for the killin'
And the Captain called, "ready, aim, fire",
Though not one of those squaddies was willin'
To refuse for them would be dire.

So ra-ta-tat-tat went the rifles,
But great uncle Burt didn't die,
For his last request, was a bullet proof vest,
And the ricochet killed Captain Bligh.

                         Tom. McDonald

Politically Correct

We must not upset Mr. Mugabee,
No, that's not because he is black,
But Dubya has told us that Saddam
Is who we all ought to attack.

If Tony commits our brave soldiers to war
To fight him and maybe to die
Remember we've seen it all happen before,
So can someone explain to us why?

For many died then and there's many who grieve,
But to send boys to war once again
How many folks are there who really believe?
That another war eases their pain?

But just think about all those plain simple folk
Who'll be victims, who don't want to die?
Or of such friendly fire that goes falling amok
From planes riding so high in the sky,

We may not have too long to wait now and see
What leaders put into effect.
But we know their decisions are certain to be
Most po-ltic-ically correct.

C.E.Beach.

August 2002

A SOLDIER OF THE GREAT WAR

A soldier of the great war
With pride stuck out his chest,
He marched away with all his mates
And by Jove, he'd do his best.

To kill as many of the enemy
As was in his power to do,
To fight for king and country,
The mighty red, white and blue.

The trenches with the duck boards flat
Against the filthy slime,
The rats that crawled around his feet,
Dead bodies caked in lime.

He felt that he was going mad,
The bombs around him falling.
The deafening noise of death so near,
The dead around him sprawling.

Thoughts of home kept him sane,
His mother's homely face.
The image of her aproned figure,
Her head bowed saying grace.

She hadn't wanted him to go,
Said he was far too young.
Eighteen meant he was now a man,
But still her only son.

The bombing started once again,
He couldn't run away.
He bowed his head and said a prayer,
To see another day.

His body was never found amid
The mud and carnage tossed
Like confetti scattered in the wind,
But this was men now lost.

Many years have passed since then,
Has man become more sane?
Did the soldier of that Great War
Die quietly in vain?

His grave is now well cared for,
Headstones where once he trod.
A soldier of the Great War
Known only unto God.

Tricia Statter

Part 3

MEMOIRS AND STORIES

WAKING THE LION by CECIL BEACH

I was born in 1926, eight years after the end of World War One in the year of the General Strike. My dad had been a staff sergeant in WW1.

Everything seemed peaceful in the sleepy Berkshire village of Didcot in 1933 when I arrived there with my parents and my baby brother Ralph. I was barely seven years old and hardly aware that Britain was still licking her wounds from WW1 and endeavouring to climb out of the recession.

I had seen the ex-service men in Oxford hanging like crows on their crutches, with trays of matches strung from their necks, being hounded along the gutters by the police. Poverty was endemic and I don't remember seeing anybody then who was fat.

I had stood in the long dole queues with my father in Oxford. He had been without regular work for eighteen months. I have seen him grey faced and trembling during a thunderstorm, suffering from the after effects of being under a barrage in Holland, during which he had crawled out to release a colleague who had been chained down in the open as a field punishment.

The country was sick of war and pacifism ruled in Britain throughout the 1930's. War had decimated the male population.

Then my Dad had walked the full fourteen and a half miles from Oxford to Didcot and back, to get work in the Didcot Royal Army Ordinance Depot. We moved into an unfinished housing estate in Didcot with clay mud roads to the front and fields to the back of the house. Then we moved again into a house provided for Depot workers inside the Depot Camp among other Depot workers, Depot Police, soldiers and their families. There was a recreation field for the children, the NAAFI, and a Civilians Club inside the camp, and a paper shop that sold sweets and comics by the guardhouse and there were fields and lanes to roam beyond them.

Apart from the odd bullies who picked on the smaller ones, life inside the camp was idyllic for the children, although in the wider world trouble was brewing. Newspapers carried stories of things being done to the Jews in Germany and Hitler had started making territorial claims.

Discussing these with my playmate George Russell, whose German mother was married to a soldier living in the camp, he told me the world's troubles were all caused by the Jews. George, was one of eight siblings with another being added yearly. They lived mostly on potato pancakes, and his mother posted parcels of butter to their relatives in Germany.

While Hitler announced more territorial claims over his nation's neighbours the British government decided to disperse parts of the Didcot Ordinance Depot, moving the clothing department and my father to work in what had been the original Branston Pickle factory at Burton-on-Trent. The factory had been built by and housed German prisoners during WW1.

Prime Minister Neville Chamberlain was playing for time, and France was getting nervous, while Hitler's troops advanced more into the countries of their European neighbours. Britain began to re-arm.

Some steps were taken to make Hitler aware of Britain's growing strength. Some of them were bluff, like the wooden or rubber inflatable battle tanks and aeroplanes that were placed to deceive passing aircraft. The arms factories moved into more production.

More cloth was being bought and tested in the Government Inspectorate of Clothing at Branston for the manufacturers of army uniforms and kilts for the Scots regiments.

In Berkshire, a few months before the start of World War Two, my dad and I watched the lights in the sky of the Aurorae Borealis. Some folks said it was a bad omen. From Burton-on-Trent years later, we watched a similar sky lighting display that was the Coventry bombings, and we wondered why none of our planes were there to intercept them. Later we learned that the defences had been held back so the Germans would not know we had tapped into and were decoding their military radio signals.

While Chamberlain continued trying to negotiate for peace, on September 1st 1939 Germany marched into Poland. Blackout and evacuation plans were put into place in Britain.

Britain and France gave Germany an ultimatum that unless Germany withdrew its forces from Poland, war would be declared. The Polish Air force collapsed under the blitzkrieg of the Luftwaffe

I was thirteen on September 3rd 1939 when I heard Neville Chamberlain broadcast from the cabinet room in 10 Downing Street that Britain was at war with Germany.

On that day a hundred and twelve people were killed when the passenger liner Athenia was sunk off Ireland by the German U-boat U-30. Then on 4th September the R.A.F attacked Germany warships in the Helgoland Bight

The Lion was Awake.

DEAR PAPA   by GRAHAM WALKER

The following letter is a fictionalised attempt, culled from original letters and World War 1 studies, to portray in all its horror the futility of War.

The theatre is Gallipoli in 1915. This was an amphibious landing from Naval Ships, of English, French, Australian, New Zealand and Indian troops on the Gallipoli Peninsula in Eastern Turkey with the intention of capturing Constantinople (now Istanbul). Allied casualties were 187,959 killed and wounded.

The 42nd East Lancashire Division was prominent in this expedition. Six Victoria Crosses were awarded for the landing on 'Lancashire Beach'. The expedition failed and troops were withdrawn on 9th January 1916 after eight months fighting.

The letter purports to be sent by a 20 year old 2nd Lieutenant to his father, also an Army Officer with a Staff Post in England.

2 weeks after writing his letter the young officer was killed.

- - - - - - - - - - - - - - -

Dear Papa,

I trust this note finds you well and coping with your staff job.

We have encountered the most dreadful ill luck, previously avoided to the extent we thought of ourselves as the favoured lucky ones. Have we tempted providence with our arrogant assumptions? It would appear so.

All we have overcome has become undone in the space of a few days and I now find myself awaiting the next misfortune, as if willing it to happen. Colonel Bob was shot dead by one of our own troopers who mistook him for a Turkish Pasha. He was carrying out a behind lines inspection wearing his French General Staff Kepi – he used to call it his lucky cap, but it proved to be not so. He was shot through the temple and died instantly.

RSM Butterworth was killed by a mine, an old one which had remained undetected but somehow, probably due to shelling and ground movement had found its way to the surface. He lost both legs and died in ten minutes. We could not staunch the blood and he had one taken off at the hip. He was quite lucid and seemed to be in not much pain and we gave him two ampoules of morphine.

As if this was not enough, a direct hit on the Communications bunker killed three officers and most of the signalling staff. The explosion caused an ammo truck to blow up and this created havoc in the rear lines. Company strength was down to 64 at day's end and we had lost 51 men, 40 killed, 11 badly wounded. I doubt if many will survive. The awful business of the day depressed us all.

Johnny Turk zeroed us in with devastating accuracy and I wonder why we were led to believe their artillery was not up to scratch. Not so, they are bloody good gunners and we are now completely pinned down. Major Graves is now Colonel and I am second in command. Not bad for a First Lieutenant one might say, but I say, how awful to receive promotion over the bodies of the fallen.

War, Papa, is a horrible business.

Good night and God Bless you my loving father.

John Smith, 2nd Lieutenant.

"MISSING PRESUMED DEAD"   by JUDY INGMAN

(From a grand-daughter's perspective)

"Missing presumed dead," now what does that mean? Well it means exactly what it says, *Missing presumed dead*, not "Missing wandering around with no memory," not "Missing, presumed alive, possibly captured" and definitely not "Missing, returning later." No, it means "Missing, presumed dead." This was the message my grandmother received in 1916, when my father had just had his first birthday.

I've often wondered, cringing inside, how she must have reacted. According to her sister, my great aunt, she screamed as she clutched the letter. I learned too, how she never really gave up hope that one day he would return. My guess is that there would be many in her position during that cruellest of wars between 1914 and 1918.

It is recorded that from Britain alone six hundred and sixty two thousand were killed, one point six million were wounded and one hundred thousand were "**Missing Presumed Dead**." The vastness of the figures makes it even harder to comprehend, so I want to discuss the impact which I believe, "Missing Presumed Dead" had on my own family.

My father was raised fatherless, an only child, whose only real male figure was his austere Victorian, maternal grandfather, who terrified him. My grandmother tried to pick up her life without her husband and to help this along, she decided to move house to start afresh nearer to her domineering father, who had agreed to help support her. Once settled there she began having doubts that maybe her beloved Alfred, (as she always referred to him) might still be alive and having recovered, return home and find her gone. This nagging worry made her restless so she and my father moved back to St Helens. Once back and seeing no return of her husband she became depressed and tried yet again to make a clean break and a fresh start. This continued throughout my father's childhood, even taking them as far as Canada on one occasion to live by her brother, for eighteen months.

My father's education suffered although he did attend the Grammar School. He learned to see to himself a lot and managed whenever possible to keep clear of the scrutiny of his grandfather. Nowhere did he receive the loving care of a man like Alfred, who was described as warm and kind-hearted.

He left school early and took on many local jobs soon showing an interest in door to door sales. My grandmother, although not elderly, suffered severely from Rheumatoid Arthritis and in latter days became confined to a wheelchair. She was understandably very possessive of her son and didn't take easily to his having girlfriends. He used to find more freedom in my great aunt's house with his younger cousin and where two doors away lived his serious girlfriend, later to become my mother.

My poor grandmother was devastated when he informed her he had enlisted in the army at the beginning of the Second World War. She was even more upset, as he was working in Ireland at the time and didn't need to join up. I can only imagine her pain at his decision; frightened that she had lost her husband to war and very possibly her son was to go the same way. From his words to us later in life, I don't think he ever realised what it meant to her. I have many times wondered if her arthritis, that was so crippling, was brought on by the stress she had undergone and fear of further loss.

My parents married in 1941 after a long courtship and I was born in 1945 near the end of the war. When my father was demobbed, we all moved to Belfast, where he had worked before the War. My sister was born a year later. My grandmother could not bear the distance and also moved to be near us. Her possessiveness interfered with a possible healthy relationship with my mother and caused friction to the marital one, too. I, being only a young infant at the time, knew none of this and loved her deeply.

My father, with an ambition fostered by his grandfather, who constantly told him he was a wastrel and would achieve nothing in life, soon changed his Sales job for a better one and after 4 years, we all moved to Yorkshire. My memories of that home are vague, but negative. It was where we all had our childhood ailments, were almost abducted by a Child Molester and where school seemed only punitive.

After more job changes for the better our final move was to Shropshire where we moved into a cottage left by an aunt on my mother's side, and for my father's job involving sales to companies rather than individuals and small shops. My grandmother managed to live a few months beside us before dying in her early sixties, with, (I've since been told), my grandfather's name on her lips.

My father without his mother became more masterful over his own family, perhaps an influence felt from his grandfather, but also I believe because he too had developed a fear over loss.

It wasn't that he was punitive or hard on us, but more that he needed to know where we were and what we were doing, even when in another room within the house. For me, as a growing youngster, rebellion was inevitable and there were many petty clashes, especially in teenage years. He had also developed my grandmother's propensity for possessiveness that makes one feel very claustrophobic. In retrospect, I am convinced that it was quite unconscious, for he was a very generous and loving man, qualities which I fantasise were inherited from his own father. Throughout his life he tried so hard to please and to better himself, a trait perhaps taken in from all the criticism from his grandfather, because he was never able to believe just how much he had achieved. He had in fact become Director of a very influential company called Multi Lift and had gained a unique tribute from Finland, where part of the company was based.

Now he has been dead these past few years, in thinking of him and his life so clearly, I miss him more and feel my understanding of him is nearer the truth.

I often wonder, if my grandfather had been killed and his body buried, whether perhaps my grandmother could have realistically let him go, and allowed herself to meet another partner and have other children. Would my father then have been less possessive? Not left us to work hard at understanding all our relationships? Trying hard to give our own children the balanced upbringing all children deserve? We will never know.

I am fully aware that his, my own and my children's childhoods and experiences of life could have been a great deal worse and it was always an upbringing based on love, although veering on over-protection. There is always an impact from the past and "**Missing Presumed Dead**" is one that I believe has dominated our lives, leaving marks that we have still not as yet been able to interpret fully.

NEAR MISSES   by ISHBEL KARGAR

Shortly before the Second World War, started my aunt married a Londoner, a kindly man with a ready smile. Uncle Maurice was a steward in the Merchant Navy, and his ship, 'Capetown Castle', like many other liners was converted to carry troops and cargo. He was away for long months, coming home with stories and unusual gifts from the legendary places he'd been visiting, South Africa, Jamaica, America, New Zealand and many others. Although the adults impressed on us that these were not pleasure cruises, we were too young to appreciate that hundreds of merchant ships were sunk in spite of sailing in convoy protected by destroyers.

The danger he was in was made real to us when he next came home on leave and showed us photographs of a sinking ship as the survivors were being helped on to the Capetown Castle. That had been a close shave. All our envious imaginings of leisurely cruises to exotic places were replaced by the reality that our dear Uncle Maurice could possibly not come home again.

- - - - - - -

The war touched our family even closer when the age limit for conscription was raised, and Dad was called up. As a builder, he became a Sapper in the Royal Engineers. His first posting was to Ballymena in Northern Ireland, for basic training, then over to Ripon where a large extension to the barracks was being built. For the rest of the war he served in various places around the country, where new military camps were being set up. Mum sometimes went to join him when he had a 48 hour leave.

One of these visits was to his posting in Chatham, just at the time the "Doodle-bugs" were being sent over to bomb London. When the air-raid warnings sounded, all the boarders were expected to go down to the cellar, or to the street shelters, but Mum and Dad had decided to take their chances by staying together in their room. (Not such a reckless decision, knowing that the street shelters were vulnerable to a direct hit, and that many cellars had been penetrated!)

Mum described the fear they felt as they heard the throb of the rocket engine flying overhead. Everyone knew that when the engine stopped, the bomb would drop straight down. People felt a guilty sense of relief when the rocket passed over and flew on, relief that they had been spared, but guilt at knowing that others were in danger.

- - - - - - -

During the blitz on Manchester, we often heard lone planes flying overhead, some dropping their load of bombs randomly as they flew home. One such missile was dropped a few streets away from our house. The next morning exciting news spread, "They've bombed the school!"

We rushed to see the ruins, excitedly savouring the weeks of 'no school' for many weeks. Alas, our joy was unfounded, the bomb had landed in the playground, the crater was already fenced in, and the few broken windows were being boarded up. Lessons continued without interruption.

THE LOVE   by CECIL BEACH

She felt her body pressed so close to his. The rough khaki fabric of his uniform almost fused against the cotton of her dress.

"Come back to me," she whispered.

He nodded smiling reassurance.

"Of course I will my darling."

They held each other in their tight embrace, ignoring the activity around them. Other couples, similarly waiting for the train moved restlessly around them.

The train pulled in hissing steam and smoke. Men poured into the carriages and turned to kiss their loves farewell.

She stood for a while after the train had gone. The platform emptied, and with tear-filled eyes she almost bumped into a porter when she began to move away.

Letters came, at first frequently, and she penned many as the time went by, not knowing where he was, but with his letters constantly assuring her that he was well. She passed her time knitting socks to send to him with her letters endorsing the love in her heart.

The bombings started. Two houses only a street away were destroyed.

He continued to write regularly to her, but was worried because he was not receiving any letters from her. At least he tried to comfort himself that he had not received one of those "Dear John" letters telling him that it was all over, as had so many of his friends.

It was months before he was able to go to see her. At last he stood on the pavement outside her home.

She had been knitting socks when the air raid warning sounded. Rather than go to the shelter, she decided to stay where she was.

She heard the sound of impact when the bomb crashed through the roof, smashing the tiles. Then the noise it made falling through the bedroom roof, then the bedroom floor. She started to move away as it landed at the side of her………………

He stared at the devastation of what had been her home for a while before he turned away, in tears.

RECOLLECTIONS OF WORLD WAR II   by JENNIFER WAITE

My name is Anne, I was a war babe and grew up in the tiny village of Gatley, near Ringway Airport which is now the dominant Manchester Airport. My father was in a reserved occupation, his firm being involved in the transportation of cotton for the manufacture of oil skins for the forces, particularly seamen. My parents were very often in Harpurhey, Manchester, where my grandparents owned an off licence.

Grannie was seriously ill with cancer and mother nursed her, whilst coping with me and we sheltered in the stillage, when the bombs dropped. I often crept down in the day time and sipped the dregs from an odd barrel poured into a tiny, orange egg cup. I remember women coming into the shop wearing shawls. Father not only held down his job, and helped his in-laws, but took turns in the Home Guard. The series "Dad's Army" fully illustrates what life was for him. Five sticks and one gun per group - all to guard Ringway Airport!

A friend of the family, whose family ran a shop-fitting service before the war, was enlisted to teach mathematics at night to service men. This was because he had been recorded as being unfit for service, but highly intelligent. Two family friends were in the fire service, one being the Chief Officer in North Wales.

The villagers of Gatley shared their resources and news of bananas, butter and sugar deliveries travelled fast. One family friend rode her bike, carrying a small bag of coal to a needy person. The women were resourceful by tending allotments. My own mother rode her bike into the Cheshire country lanes and purchased fruit for jamming and bottling. I accompanied her, strapped into a home-made wooden seat made by my father.

On the landing at home, stood a tall single utility wardrobe, fully shelved, where my mother kept her supplies under lock and key! She was adept at creating meals – glazed eggs, brawn from pigs' brains, rabbit stew. We ate salted beans from earthenware jars, now housing my kitchen utensils! Neighbours lent one another cups full of sugar, a product we take for granted now, at least until an emergency.

Milk was distributed free to school children, in small 1/3 pint bottles, (the temperature of the milk varied according to the weather (no fridges in schools then)). Beige ration books were issued from the local office of the Ministry of Food in nearby Cheadle. There concentrated orange juice was available for toddlers and dried milk (Ostermilk in purple tins), was used by the new baby next door. This was the age of the bronze three-penny bit, the farthing and the silver sixpence.

I remember my Mickey-Mouse gas mask and the shared air raid shelter which still stands to this day with its thick cement block roof. Dad later converted his share into an organised tool shed. Toys were scarce. People exchanged toys or made their own. One Christmas, Dad made me a large, deep pink, doll's cot and I had a beautiful black, second hand dolls pram. He also made me wooden jigsaws using a fretsaw of large pictures he had been given. Recycling was essential. My mother was also adept at utilizing materials – shirt flaps became aprons with bright colourful sashes and large pockets. I remember Mum's old coat being transformed into a smart dressing gown for me.

Despite the war, my mother made Christmas wonderful for me – homemade paper decorations, conserves preserved for a cake- I am sure mother often went without, and we made home produced Christmas cards, calendars and gifts. My aunt, Dad's younger sister lived in Stretford. She had contacts in the grocery trade and I remember Auntie Kerry who lived until she was 101, wrapping up ¼lb. of tea as Dad's Christmas present. Each Christmas, my father's two sisters plus my mother gave a family party – somehow they managed to meet up to share Christmas. Strong ties persisted long after the war. Sadly the organisers are deceased, but as the youngest member of the family I had a marvellous time and remember it all to this day. What happy recollections!!

Jennifer Waite (AJW)

THE HOME FRONT   by JEAN M GIDMAN

Neither of my two grandfathers fought in World War 1. My paternal grandfather, John Perkins, was born on 12 February 1872 and was therefore 42 when war was declared. It was not, however, only his age which caused him not to go to the front, He was a coal miner in the West Yorkshire Coalfield at Garforth. As coal was needed for the war effort he was exempt. He helped to keep the home fires burning.

My maternal grandfather, Ernest Moverley, though younger than John Perkins, being born on 22 June 1885, had been a farmer with his own farm since the age of 16. He was 29 when the war broke out, He farmed at Little Langton Grange near Northallerton in North Yorkshire. He was called up and went to Catterick Camp. When the recruiting sergeant heard that he was a farmer with his own farm, and not a farm labourer, he was told to go home and he would be sent for when needed. He never was. However the war did come to his door.

Because of the shortage of farm labourers he employed a Belgian refugee for a while. I regret that I do not know his name but he was a wood carver by trade and made some beautifully carved furniture for my grandmother, some of which I still have. He was not a joiner and therefore it is screwed together not dovetailed. I don't know the exact period he was on the farm but he dated some of the pieces with 1916 (the year of my mother's birth). While these heirlooms remain with the family the war will not be forgotten.

THE FORGOTTEN FRONT

It was not until I started doing the family history that my husband, John, produced his cousin's medals from World War 1. John had been given them during World War 2, when his uncle Tom, who had been bombed out from his home, had given them to John's father Alfred, for John as both John's were Sergeants. They are the Service Medals, The British War Medal 1914-1920 and the Victory Medal. Engraved round the rim is "37001 Sgt. J.Gidman Manch. Reg." We knew he had died in the War but did not where or how. We wrote to the Ministry of Defence to see if they had any information but the records had been destroyed during World War 2.

We eventually found the information in "Soldiers Killed in World War 1". He died of wounds on 10 January 1917 in Mesopotamia. When he died he was with the 1st battalion of the Manchester Regiment, but he had originally enlisted in the Liverpool Regiment. On looking at the Commonwealth War Graves website we found that he was buried at the Amara War Cemetery in Iraq.

From research that Richard Houghton has done it would appear that John Gidman enlisted in the Kings Liverpool Regiment sometime in late 1915 or early 1916. It is unlikely that he served in France. He was subsequently transferred to the Manchester Regiment and ended up in Mesopotamia.

On obtaining his birth certificate we found that he was born on 15 October 1895 which means that he was 21 years old when he died.

The cemetery was originally laid out with individual gravestones but the sand corroded the stones and they were eventually removed and a monument listing all the dead replaced them.

I called this the forgotten front. But why were British soldiers fighting so far away?

By the end of the 19th Century the Ottoman Empire was crumbling and, in an attempt to maintain its eastern borders, joined the Triple Alliance in order to reduce the risk of invasion from Russia. In doing so it put the oil fields of Persia which were jointly owned with Britain at risk and in order to defend them the British Army in India was sent to Mesopotamia. It easily controlled Basra and Amara and then continued up the Tigris towards Kut. It took Kut but was then besieged by Turkish troops in the spring of 1916, finally surrendering in April. The Turks then occupied it and the next year was spent trying to retake Kut prior to pushing on to Baghdad. Armara was used as a hospital facility which was how John Gidman came to die there.

My husband, John, never knew his cousin who had died before he was born. We still have the medals and with them the memory of Sergeant John Gidman.

ROCKING THE RAFTERS   by VALERIE ROCHE

One job Jimmy didn't like was bagging up potatoes; Or rather it wasn't so much the job as the place he had to do it in. It was in a musty smelling barn behind the farm shop, a dark, crumbly building, which creaked and groaned in the wind. Chains and ropes rattled and swayed from the beams up above.

Tom, the regular farm hand, teased him when he said he didn't like being in the building, "Ay, that'll be on account of the ghost, lad!"

"Ghost! There's no such thing as ghosts. I just meant I don't like it because it's so cold and dark, even on a summer's day!"

"Never seen anything myself lad, but the place definitely gives me the creeps – because of the old ghost story."

Jimmy laughed, "Oh, you're just winding me up Tom."

Tom shook his sandy head, "No! It's a true story, from the First World War about a young lad who was working here. At the time, lads had flocked to volunteer to fight the Germans, many of them under-age. Madness it was. Whole villages joined up together and were wiped out together. The Pals they were called."

"What was the lad's name?"

"Daniel." Tom stood with his hands in his pockets, legs apart gazing down at his steel toe-capped boots.

"Well?"

"Well what?"

"What happened to him?"

"Well, he wasn't like you Jimmy, he wouldn't volunteer. He said he didn't want to kill anyone, didn't want to die in some foreign land, which he'd never seen, for a cause no one could explain to him. Joining up wasn't compulsory until eighteen, so he couldn't be forced to, but they made him suffer."

"They, who were they?"

"The people from the village, women mostly. Even when conscription began in 1916 he was only sixteen. When he didn't try to sneak in under-age they sneered at him and called him a coward."

Jimmy was outraged, "That was his decision. He wasn't even old enough!"

"Not in the eyes of the villagers then. Many of them had already lost their boys who signed up illegally, some as young as fourteen. They didn't see why anyone else should get away with it. People began to shun him and turned their backs on him in the street.

They refused to speak to him, even spat at him and painted a hangman's noose on the front door of his parent's house. They made his mother so ill that she almost died."

"Yes, but what happened to him?"

"He was found hanging from the top beam of the barn. No-one knows if he was murdered or he hung himself, with the persecution, you know."

Jimmy shuddered thinking of all the time he had spent in the barn alone.

"How come you know all this?"

"He belonged to our family lad." Tom turned and walked across the yard.

Jimmy sensed Tom's sadness, even though he didn't show it, but it didn't stop him calling out after him, "Thanks a lot Tom! Now I have to go in there and work on my own!"

Jimmy had worked in the barn many times since Tom's revelations, always with the comfort of the radio playing his favourite rock music. Despite Jimmy's protestations of not believing in ghosts, the place still gave him the creeps and loud rock music helped anaesthetise his brain. The rafters were rattling away to the sound of the Kings of Leon "Your sex is on Fire" with Jimmy weighing potatoes in time to the music when silence hit the barn like a cruise missile. Jimmy's heart lurched. The silence was such a shock. He picked up his radio and fiddled with the aerial and the tuner, but he couldn't get it to work. He unplugged it and examined the mains connection, but couldn't find anything obviously wrong with it. Jimmy cursed to himself, thinking it must be the fuse in the plug, and wished he'd brought batteries. "I'll just have to do without for now," he thought, and shivered involuntarily.

Jimmy continued to work alone and with only an hour before 'knocking off time', he determined to stick it out. He thought he could hear a rustling sound from above but looking up, could see nothing. Several times he heard the noise but couldn't see anything and assumed it was a wood pigeon or a mouse scuffling, at least that's what he hoped it was.

At home time, Jimmy picked up his radio and with some relief walked out of the barn, jumped on his bike and rode out of the yard. He stopped at the garage, bought batteries and then cycled home. After his tea he went up to his room and tested the radio with the batteries and then with the mains. "I don't get it," he thought. "It's working fine now and that's a new socket in the barn. Oh well, I'll try it again tomorrow". The thought of another day in the barn alone made him shudder so he decided to go down to the Ship Inn to meet some of his mates.

Heading for the bathroom, passing his sister's room, he looked in, to ask how her exams were going but she wasn't there. He turned to leave but a familiar rustling sound made him look back. He saw the pages of a book flickering in the breeze from the open window. He went over to close the window and picked up the book. 'World War 1 – A History for GCSE.' "It's just a coincidence," he thought, but he felt uneasy just the same.

Next day Jimmy went to work in the barn again. He plugged in the radio and it worked immediately. Within a short while he was back in the swing of things, working away and dreaming of the day when he'd be a soldier as he had longed to be since he was a boy.

"Promise me you'll at least do your 'A' levels first Jimmy before you join up," his mother had said and he had agreed reluctantly.

Now and again his eyes would be drawn to look up at the rafters, but there was nothing to see – to his relief! Then it began!

First the radio stopped just like the day before, but this time to Freddie Mercury's "Who wants to live for ever?" The resultant silence was oppressive and absolute, yet deafening. Jimmy couldn't hear a bird, the wind, anything except his own pounding heart, until the rustling sound started again, and he remembered his sister's room the night before.

"It sounds like a book, the pages of a book, but where is it?" Jimmy looked up towards the rafters afraid of what he might see, relieved still to see nothing. His head began to pound and he felt dizzy. His heart thumped so loud he thought it must be heard by the whole world. Then from somewhere inside himself he heard, "Help me Jimmy. Help me tell the truth please!" Jimmy felt as if his head and his chest would burst and his legs wouldn't hold him up as he held onto a wooden bar and gasped, "Who are you? What do you want?"

A voice, this time from the depths of the velvety blackness of the barn answered him, "I'm Daniel, Daniel Hanson. Help me tell the truth – come up here!"

No way thought Jimmy, but he couldn't believe what his body was doing. He was walking towards the ladder and he couldn't stop. He had no choice. He felt and saw his arms and legs climbing the rickety ladder and could do nothing about it. The back of his throat was dry and swollen. He opened his mouth to cry out but no sound came. All the time he could hear the rustling of the pages of a book, "Go on Jimmy, keep going! Don't fail me please!"

He reached the top of the ladder and collapsed on the loft floor. He looked over the edge to the floor of the barn. The ground seemed to surge up towards him. He managed to get to his feet and immediately regretted it. Nauseous with fear and nerves all he could do was sway and sweat, rooted to the spot. Jimmy hated heights at the best of times and this was the worst of times.

There was a sudden flash of light making Jimmy look up. Before him, gradually coming into focus, appeared the wretched tear-tracked face of a young girl, reaching out to him. Next he saw an older woman sobbing and wringing her apron in her hands. With an overwhelming feeling of sadness and despair, he saw a crowd of women jeering and shaking their fists, whilst others turned their backs. Something landed at his feet and although he could not see it he knew it was a stone. He was falling, or at least he felt as if he was and he grabbed a rope to steady himself. He heard the voice again, "Help me tell the truth Jimmy!"

He had no idea what he was supposed to be doing but he began searching frantically, overturning things and rummaging through discarded items. He could hear himself mumbling out loud, but as if from a distance.

"Daniel, if you're there, I don't know what I'm looking for? Show me!"

At once a ray of light shone from behind Jimmy and rested on a cross section of the rafters in front of him. He stood transfixed and stared as before him appeared the horrifying sight of the body of a young man, his face livid with strangulation, eyes popping and tongue lolling, swinging from a rope lashed to the rafters. Jimmy's stomach turned, his legs buckled and his head swam then for the first time in his life, he fainted.

When he came to seconds later, the dreadful sight was gone and standing before him was the living image of Daniel Hanson, looking down at him concerned.

"I'm sorry Jimmy. I didn't mean to frighten you!" Then he faded away, blended into the background. Silence reigned and then the rustling of the pages began again. Jimmy looked up into the shaft of light and there on the rafter he could see the pages of a book fluttering in the draught. He stood up and dragged over a box, climbed on top and managed to stretch the tips of his fingers to the book. He pulled it clear and the box wobbled under him sending him crashing to the floor of the loft. Jimmy sat up and looked at the cover of the book from which he read out loud, "The journal of Molly Dickens 1916."

He did not remember descending the ladder, but found himself walking towards the door of the barn, the journal tucked in the belt of his jeans. The sun was glaringly bright and a comfort after the oppressive gloom and chill of the barn, but nothing could clear away the images he had seen. The voice of Daniel rang round and round in his head. He must get home. He found his bike and cycled home. Telling his Mum he had a headache he climbed into bed and slept until it was dark.

When Jimmy woke he went downstairs and heated his dinner in the microwave. He sat at the table to read Molly's journal. The address inside read, "The Vicarage" and Jimmy assumed Molly was the vicar's daughter. Gradually the story of her situation was revealed as Jimmy read on until he came to this entry:

May 16th 1916. I fear the worst. The curse has not yet come and is late by one week. If I am with child what will I do. William is home next week but I love Daniel so! Father would never allow me to marry a younger son and William would kill Daniel if he knew what we have been doing.

So Daniel and Molly were up to no good eh! Poor William! Jimmy read on:

May 22nd 1916. The whole world is crumbling around me. William came home yesterday. What a state he is in, so badly hurt and shaking constantly. I knew I could not tell him about Daniel and me, for he clung to me and cried so for the things he had witnessed. He said I was all that had kept him going. How could we have done this? I caught up with Daniel and told him we must finish and that I could not break William's heart. He begged me to change my mind and when I said I couldn't he ran from me and no one has seen him for hours. No one else knows why though and not a living soul knows what I fear, that I am pregnant.

May 23rd 1916. They found Daniel today, cut him down from a rope in the old barn. Oh Daniel! I wish I were dead too!

There were no entries after that. "Molly must not have had the heart to write again", thought Jimmy.
Next day Jimmy was at work early and went to see Tom, taking the journal. He told him what had happened the day before and Tom listened open-mouthed. Placing the journal in his hands Jimmy told him what he had read.
"Molly Dickens was my great-grandmother and William Hanson was my great-grandfather." Tom said. "She must have passed off her first child John – my Grandad as William's son. So Daniel was my real great-grandfather!"

"That must be what he was trying to tell us and that he lives on in your branch of the family. I guess we'll never know if he was murdered or he took his own life. It could have been that Molly's rejection was the last straw, and on top of the persecution he couldn't face watching the woman he loved live her life with his brother."

Tom nodded, "No, we'll never know now but at least we know who he really was."

Tom and Jimmy walked over to the barn and entering they felt the familiar cold, unfriendly atmosphere.

"Daniel, can you still hear me?" Jimmy called out. ""We know the truth now, your family know about you and Molly. You can go in peace now, Daniel!"

Jimmy began to recite the Lord's Prayer and Tom joined in, their heads bowed. The icy cold atmosphere began to thaw and melted into a comfortable warmth blending with the hot June day.

"No one else needs know about this Tom, just you, Daniel and me, if you'd rather have it that way."

"Thanks Jimmy, I'd be grateful, at least until I talk it over with the family." said Tom.

"That's the way it'll be then Tom."

Tom walked away, journal in hand. Jimmy looked around the barn, up at the rafters, saw nothing and felt relieved.

"I think it's time to get back to work, Daniel!"

He plugged his radio in and the air was filled with the sound of U2's "It's a beautiful day". Unlike Daniel, Jimmy looked forward to the day he would be joining up but for now there were potatoes to bag up.

THE KAISER IN THE LAKE DISTRICT   by RON BLACK

In the years leading up to the Great War, the then German Kaiser Wilhelm II visited Lakeland on a number of occasions from 1895 onward, staying with Lord Lonsdale and touring the district as well as cruising on Lake Ullswater. For one of his visits, the Raven had her decks painted yellow and was used as a Royal Yacht. The Raven still sails Ullswater today.

There is a story that on one of his ascents of the Kirkstone Pass in the early 1900's, Joe Bowman the famous Ullswater huntsman (who had a fox gone to ground in one of the Dove Crag borrans) looked down and upon seeing the procession was reputed to have said "I'd like to strangle yon fella and bury him among these rocks" Perhaps he had a premonition about the coming war.

Beatrix Potter also watched the procession and recorded the following entry in her diary.

"Tuesday August 15th 1895. We consumed three whole hours waiting to see the Emperor, not very well worth it. I had seen him in London. I think he is stouter. I was not particularly excited. I think it is disgraceful to drive fine horses like that. First came a messenger riding a good roan belonging to Bowness, which we could hear snorting before they came in sight, man and horse both dead-beat. He reported the Emperor would be up in ten minutes, but it was twenty.

The procession consisted of a mounted policeman with a drawn sword in a state approaching apoplexy, the red coats of the Quorn Hunt, four or five of Lord Lonsdale's carriages, several hires and spare horses straggling after them. There were two horses with an outside rider to each carriage, splendid chestnuts thoroughbreds floundering along and clinking their shoes.

They were not going fast when we saw them, having come all the way from Patterdale without even stopping at Kirkstone to water the horses, to the indignation of mine host, and an assembly of three or four hundred who had reckoned on this act of mercy.

I think his majesty deserved an accident and rather wonder he didn't have one considering the smallness of the little Tiger sitting on the box to work the break.

The liveries were blue and yellow and the carriages much yellow singularly ugly low tub. With a leather top to shut up sideways. The Emperor, Lord Lonsdale and two ladies in the first, Lady Dudley etc in the second.

There was a considerable crowd and very small flags. German ones bad to get at short notice, but plenty of tricolours. Lord Lonsdale is red headed and has a harum-scarum reputation, but according to Mr Edmondson, less "stupid" than his predecessor whom he had seen "Beastly droonk" in the road on a Sunday morning

The Kaiser also shot deer in the nearby Martindale Deer Forest and a large bungalow was constructed for him and his entourage in the 1880s. This same bungalow is available today as a holiday let. On one occasion, the Kaiser and his retinue travelled over the Kirkstone Pass, the horses being well lathered on arrival at their destination, apparently. My grandfather and two of my great uncles went to see him pass by. One of my great uncles told me the tale ending with the words "but we never thowt (thought) we'd be fighting the bugger".

A STUDY IN WAR.   by KEITH VENABLES

The year was 1916. The Great War still raged across the channel. They hadn't expected it to go on this long, nearly two years now. They said it would be over by Christmas but it still continued and young men were constantly being urged to join the forces. "Your Country needs you", was the much repeated advertising slogan used.   Most of the young men Jimmy knew had already enlisted.   Industry and agriculture were becoming desperate for workers and many women had gone to work in factories, on the land and even in the mines.

Jimmy contemplated the future. He was sitting eating his snap at the coal face beside his older brother, Charlie. They had both followed their father and grandfather into the mines.   There was little else to do in South Yorkshire, then.   Most young men ended up down the pit, even some women patriotically replaced the many men who had enlisted.

He thought as he ate, how exciting it must be to share the camaraderie of the military family, to engage in battle, to drive the enemy back and win honour for the regiment.   How exciting it would be to have a medal pinned on his breast and return home a hero.

"A penny for them lad."
"What," cried Jimmy, startled by the voice in his ear.
"Your thoughts boy, a penny for them." It was Charlie. "I've spoken to thee twice and tha's said nowt."
"I'm sorry," responded James. "I was just thinking. I'm fed up working here in this muck." He paused. "I'd like to enlist like Billy."
"Tha'd better not let ar' Mam hear thee.   She went ballistic when I told her I'd signed on.   Anyway tha's too young, tha's only sixteen."
"Johnny Walsh is no older than me and they accepted him last week," retorted Jimmy.
"Forget it," snapped Charlie,   "Get back to work or t' Gaffer'll be after thee."

With that comment, the conversation ended but having expressed his intention, James kept the thought in his mind.   He needed some excitement, not this filthy job day in day out.

****

James sat on the submerged duckboard knee deep in freezing mud, in a waterlogged trench near the area known as the Somme. He thought of home, of his Mam, Dad and sister. He knew they would be thinking and praying for him and his brother at the local chapel. It was rare that any mail got through but he knew he was not forgotten. He could see them now and recalled the anger, distress and pain they felt when he had left home to join his regiment at Richmond. His Mam was almost in a state of collapse. She had already said a tearful goodbye to one of her sons and now her baby was following him to war. What a fool he had been to leave his Mam. She would be by a huge warm fire thinking of him in his soggy uniform. It never seemed to stop raining and he couldn't get his feet warm. This was sheer hell.

They were told that at seven thirty hours, they would be going over the top. He was terrified. The last time he had been over the top, he had charged with his mates through a hail of deadly fire. All around him, enemy shells had screamed through the air, carrying death for many. He had seen shells explode nearby making the ground shake like an earthquake. Some of his mates had been buried alive in the miasma of mud and filth, but they couldn't stop to dig them out. It was so wasteful. Sometimes they gained a few yards, only to lose it next day.

It should be easier this time. Thousands of tons of explosives had been rained on the enemy trenches. Nobody could have lived through that lot. Soon the nightmare would be over.

The time approached. A whistle blew and many thousands of British and Allied soldiers swarmed over the top. They didn't know that the enemy were housed in underground concrete bunkers and so were largely unscathed by the barrage. As the Allied soldiers slowly advanced they were scythed down by relentless machine gun fire. Wave after wave of men met the same fate. Within the first few hours, twenty six thousand men and boys lay dead and by the end of the day a further eighty odd thousand of their comrades were also dead or severely wounded. Some got back to their lines, Charley was not among them. The survivors felt the pain which would never go away, but they were too numb and exhausted to mourn. Eventually an Armistice was reached. The blood bath was over.

For months, Jimmy lay in hospital trying to recover from the trauma of battle. Most of his wounds would heal but there was little hope for his lungs. His Granddad had retired early from the pit, hardly able to breathe as his lungs were full of coal dust. Jimmy had escaped that but he could barely breathe because his lungs were burned by gas. He walked with a stick having lost several toes, through frostbite.

Now he was travelling home, a little older and much wiser. Britain and the Allies had won, only it didn't feel like it. He was dreading the family reunion. Whatever the future held, the pain and nightmares would always be there. Things would never be the same again for the whole family. No one can pass through war without being scarred, even if those scars are not visible.

EVACUEES   by ISHBEL KARGAR

When War was declared, shortly before my 10th birthday, children living in large towns or near industrial areas were evacuated to the countryside away from possible bombing raids. Most children went as school parties, together with their teachers, and were somehow absorbed into the local village schools, the evacuees being billeted with local families.

At morning Assembly one day, the headmaster called for silence.

"Children, the school is going to be evacuated to the countryside very soon. Your teachers will give each of you a special paper to take home. Ask your parents to read it carefully, and if they want you to come away with the school they must sign the form and send it back to me. The children not going away will attend classes with children from other schools who are also staying behind"

Over the next few days the assembly hall was full of children collecting their small green rucksacks in which to pack their snacks and small personal items for the journey.

I desperately wanted one of those rucksacks, and was bitterly disappointed when my mother refused to sign the consent form. Nevertheless when it was the turn of my class to go to the assembly hall, I went along and joined the queue. The teacher asked for the consent form and I told her I hadn't brought it. However, she gave me a rucksack and told me to bring the form next day. Mum was cross when I showed her my precious bag.

"No Ishbel, you're not going away, you're staying here with us. We are miles away from anything the Germans would want to bomb!" (Actually, we were only a mile or so from AVRO, a complex of factories, which we later learned were making armaments and aircraft parts).

I was in a sulk the next day when she took me to the headmaster's room to return the rucksack.

A few days later I joined a few other children as we watched the evacuees board the coaches, with their lovely green rucksacks on their backs, and name labels tied to their coats. Though many of the mothers were crying, I still resented being left behind.

Several of the children came back after a few weeks, some with stories of the hard times they'd had, as unwelcome guests in overcrowded country cottages, or helping on farms, and I realised I'd probably had a lucky escape.

Later in the war I had joined the Girl Guides, and our troop was sent to the local chapel to help with evacuees arriving from London, escaping the Blitz. The buses arrived, and a tired-looking crowd made their way into the hall, mainly children, some with their mothers but most were unaccompanied. They were welcomed by WVS members and other helpers. We entertained the children, distributing sandwiches and drinks, and trying to make them feel welcome, though most of them were so tired and bewildered, they only needed to sleep after their long journey to Lancashire, so we helped to set out rows of trestle beds in a quiet room. Eventually the hall cleared, all the evacuees having been allocated to local families for safe keeping.

My own family had taken in a family of children from the East End of London. Young Eileen Parker and her brother Teddy were billeted with Aunty Sylvia and Grandma, their brother Billy moved in with us, and Tommy, another brother, was placed with family close by.

These children were totally bewildered by the sudden change in their young lives, and we tried to help them settle in. Initially we found it hard to understand what they were saying. The strong Cockney accent was so strange for us, and of course they probably had the same difficulty in understanding our Lancashire dialect.

One particular phrase became a family saying in later years. We took the children for a walk through the woods and out to the fields which surrounded the council estate, and Eileen exclaimed, "See! Ceyars in a feeyood, o'sis an 'o!" This translated as "Cows in a field, horses and all!" Coming from the built-up areas around the Docks, seeing those animals roaming free in the fields, they probably felt they'd been transported to another world.

FAMILY MEMORIES   by LYNN LAWTON

WW1

My paternal grandmother (Jane Stubbs ,a headmistress then) passed away before my parents were married in 1933 and my Grandad (James Stubbs) passed away when I was 4. Although he did survive the war, he died from the after effects of having been gassed.

However, one anecdote from that period related to me was when my grandmother was expecting Grandad home on leave from the trenches. She was preparing for his home coming.

Food was in short supply and thinking to give him a treat, she bought a tin of bully beef. But my poor grandfather's thought, when served with it, was that this was all they been eating all the time they were in the trenches! Poor grandmother! After all her efforts to make his leave a welcoming one.

WW2

My father, Edward James Stubbs, was too old to be called up, so he remained in a reserved occupation as principal of his family firm in St Helens - Grayson and Burrows - (we moved to live in Ormskirk some time after the War).

When his male employees were called up, he made up their army pay to a suitable salary for the length of the War. All his employees also had a non-contributory pension. I think he was a man ahead of his time.

He continued to run his business with the help of a single female cousin, a single lady and a retired gentleman until the end of the war. He retained all those who had served him during the War and when, fortunately, the men returned, they got their old jobs back. Many of the men who had served in the forces were not so fortunate to come back to employment.

I attach a photograph of him proudly wearing his Home Guard uniform. He was the first man in St Helens to enlist in the Home Guard, after hearing on the radio the announcement of the formation of the Home Guard. He went to the local Police station to sign up and they knew nothing about it! My mother recalled cosseting his evening meal until late on in the night until he came off duty, only to hear him tell of how the local farmers (also in the Home Guard) had brought generous suppers with them, which they shared out amongst everyone in the platoon!

One of my mother's reminiscences was of when Britain stood alone against the threat of invasion from Hitler's army. The women were buying up the stocks of pepper to arm themselves to "fight in the streets". This would have possibly been their only means of self defence for themselves and their families. Improvisation was truly the watchword in those dark days.

The church halls of St Helens were used as refuges for the evacuees from the Liverpool Blitz. One night my Aunty Chris was helping out in one and was concerned to see a little old lady weeping. Thinking she might have lost her family or even her home in the bombing, she went over to her to console her, only to learn that the stoical "Scouser" was crying for the loss of "all those lovely pubs in Scottie Road (Scotland Road)". So those were her priorities during the blitz!!!

Another memory from my mother was that, during the days of strict rationing, households were only allowed one egg a week per person. She gave hers to my sister (born in 1939). She told me that although she would have liked more children then (I was born later) she took the difficult decision not to have any more at that time as it would have been one more mouth to feed at a time when the nation faced near starvation, and also fearing the worst, bringing another child into a world possibly dominated by the Nazis. A truly responsible attitude to parenthood that many potential parents of today could learn from.

A barter economy existed then. When my mother was getting desperate for food for my sister she went to someone whom she thought was a friendly neighbour, who kept chickens, to ask for an egg, only to be refused and to be told that it was because Mum didn't have anything to offer in return! So much for the wartime spirit that successive generations have, maybe over sentimentally, infused that time with.

I do hope these few thoughts that I have recalled and tried to retain over the years, from those not to be forgotten periods in Britain's history, will be of some interest. It has given me the much delayed opportunity to put them down in writing and some not inconsiderable satisfaction in doing so.

EDWIN'S STORY   by PATRICK WAITE

Edwin stood at the base of Ypres (Menin Gate) Memorial looking up at Panel 3 searching for his uncle's name. No.1548, he had been one of 54,000 officers and men whose graves are not known, and had died aged 19 on Friday 30th October 1914. Edwin's son had visited the Memorial earlier in the year with his school history group and had given them the task of finding the name for No. 1548.

"Look, sir, there is your surname," said one of his pupils but it was on the wrong side of the family. Looking higher up and FEAH was there. The name was there, but killed in action as a member of the Household Cavalry and Cavalry of the Line, Royal Horse Guards (the Blues). Where and How?

In their book, 'Cameos of the Western Front Ypres Sector 1914-1918', Spagnoly and Smith discuss activities at Zandvoorde which was held by the 7th Cavalry Brigade with Lord Worsley's Trench on the 30th October 1914. The rudimentary trench "*was held by dismounted cavalry facing the enemy...the Household Cavalry in their new role as infantry...the 27year old Lord Worsley, a machine gun officer of the Royal Horse Guards had spent seven days and nights in the trench with his men... not prepared for the onslaught that would thunder down on the 30th. Germans opened a devastating bombardment ... Horse Guards suffered almost total extinction; ten men got back but all remaining officers and other ranks were listed as missing. The British Cavalry men vacated the area leaving their dead comrades in a now German occupied sector of the Flanders battlefield.*" Was FAEH there?

Edwin remembers a very large framed coloured photograph in the family home, of his two uncles, and now he has the said photograph on loan. It shows them in ceremonial uniform on horseback probably at Windsor prior to the beginning of the war. One can only imagine what my grandparents felt on receiving it as a gift! What else remains of this young life 100 years later?

Well, a Territorial Force Army Form E 501 listing personal details which shows he was a member of the Territorial Army in 28.06.11, prior to enrolling in the Regular Army as a Special Reserve recruit in 18.11.12 and as a member of the Expeditionary Force.

His name appears variously as Edward, Ed or Edwin aged 18 with a height and physical details the same as Edwin's!

However there are Memorandum addressed to his mother which show that on 11.07.16 there was a list of articles left by No.1548 including:

"*3 Serge Jackets, 3 Tunics, 5 Pairs of overalls, 2 Pairs Riding Pants*"... with a note that *"the government price of the articles, if sold now would amount to nineteen shillings and nine pence. If sold amongst his comrades after the war, a larger amount would probably be realised. Will you inform me as to the steps you wish to be taken?. Quartermaster I/C Records RHG."'*

His mother's answer dated 24th Sept. 1916 is interesting to say the least. "*The price the Government offers for my Boy's Uniform is scandalous seeing the price the same Government charged him for them, also where is his white leather breeches also white gauntlets and there was a lot more things...I think the best thing to do is to take what is offered...*'

The reply to this was received on 26th Sept 1916 and stated "*The price is fixed by the government*", but noted that "*he received an allowance and further, if he was a careful soldier, he would probably save his clothing allowance. Leather breeches and white gauntlets are not the property of the soldier, but are supplied and maintained by the government.*"

His mother's letter of 27th Nov.1916 asked "*to let us have the money, we have not received it yet kindly oblige as soon as possible.*" Edwin's thoughts on Trooping of the Colours reflect these observations!

This story reflects the ensuing effects of the death of Edwin No.1548 and I suddenly realised, in June 2014, that this was the reason I had the middle Christian name of Edwin. My maternal Grandparents died in 1940 and 1942 and I was born in 1941. No other family member ever discussed my middle Christian name formerly hidden in confused Government Papers. Mystery solved or is it, for one uncle?

The second uncle in the picture, the elder, has his own story which 100 years later is still being investigated. He lies in a lone war grave at Aix en Issart, awarded the DCM in May 1915, and killed by a live bomb while demonstrating to comrades behind friendly lines. I also have a cousin's family of which I have never seen or heard. Such are the effects of war.

Another mystery, why was there an Interflora dead flower on his grave when we last visited? I wish to acknowledge the research being undertaken by Richard Houghton, Secretary of the Lathom and Burscough Military Heritage Society on our behalf, so that one day soon, more of my uncle's last days will be known by Edwin the younger.

WOMEN AT WAR   by KEITH VENABLES.

A great deal of discussion has ensued about the merits or demerits of allowing ourselves to be embroiled in the Great War. Many feel it was essential, despite the cost in human lives. Others express their belief that the cost was much too high and therefore we should never have got involved. The cost was excessive. Almost a whole generation of young men died in the conflict or were irreparably damaged for what remained of their lives, to say nothing of the German losses. But be that as it may, the Great War was fought with all its' consequences.

Up to that point, life was clearly defined for both genders. A man's role was to be the bread winner, marry and provide for his family by whatever means his gifts prescribed, subject to status. In high society, inheritance of estate wealth and title fell to the eldest son. The second son went into the Church, following a career in the Priesthood, or he took a commission in the forces.

The lower orders followed a "trade" marketing their skills as salesmen, gardeners, factory workers, farm hands etc. Perhaps at the bottom of society come the labourers, navvies as they were known in the days of my youth. Indeed, much of England's wealth and industry was built on the backs of the nameless men at the bottom of society.

Women too had their roles clearly defined and followed pre-ordained paths. High Society Ladies lived lives of wasteful indulgence having unseen maids and servants to do everything for them, even dressing, undressing and washing. Their plan in life was to make a good marriage to a wealthy man. Girls from the lower classes were largely encouraged to aim for domestic work as maid servants or to running a household and childbearing, if she could find a husband who gave her security.

But the Great War was to change all that. Of course, war was not women's work, but almost an entire generation of young men were across the channel in France or Belgium and elsewhere, fighting under the most appalling conditions, with poor leadership and few resources. This was a war of attrition affecting every nation on Earth. Back at home, workers were desperately needed to do the many tasks that keep a nation operational.

The home fires must be kept burning. Only females were available to perform the many tasks that were necessary to keep the nation afloat. Women from all classes of society wanted to serve their country and support their menfolk in the war effort. Some learned to drive buses, trams, vans etc.

Many women flooded into the factories and worked all hours making and shipping ordnance for the front, to keep the armed forces equipped with the resources required to fight the foe. Many worked as nurses rebuilding shattered bodies and lives, in hospitals, both back home and in the field. Yet others drove ambulances ferrying crippled soldiers from the front line, with the most appalling wounds back to the field hospitals, often under enemy fire. They saw sights and endured dangers that no one should ever have to face.

Of course, throughout history, in every generation females have proved that they are the equal of males in courage, endurance, fortitude and toughness. I recall as a child, reading of a very tough sergeant who, over many years, had risen through the ranks in perhaps the toughest of fighting forces, the French Foreign Legion. Eventually the sergeant died in a skirmish, in a riff ambush. It was only then the doctors learned that the sergeant was a woman.

Throughout all wars, women have displayed amazing courage, often laying down their lives, dicing with death on a daily basis, in clandestine warfare as undercover agents. Sometimes even in the front line alongside their male counterparts.

The Great War finally ended but things could not return as they were. The "gears" of national life resumed their daily grind. However, there were not enough able bodied men to meet the needs of industry. Alternatively, having experienced a measure of freedom, women were unwilling to tamely return to their former prescribed roles. Real emancipation and equality for women had not yet arrived. There were still many steps to take before that could be achieved, but of necessity, the Great War had provided a major step forward, that could never be retracted.

If I may quote some verses from a much longer poem by Rudyard Kipling,

The Female of the Species.

When the Himalayan peasant meets the he bear in his pride,
He shouts to scare the monster, who will sometimes turn aside.
But the she bear thus accosted rends the peasant tooth and nail.
For the female of the species is more deadly than the male.

But the woman that God gave him, every fibre of her frame
Proves her launched for one sole issue, armed and engined for the same,
And to serve that single issue, lest the generations fail,
The female of the species must be deadlier than the male.

And Man knows it! Knows, moreover, that the woman that God gave him
Must command but may not govern - shall enthral but not enslave him.
And she knows, because she warns him, and her instincts never fail,
For the female of her species is more deadly than the male.

MURPHY, THE DONKEY   by PATRICIA STATTER

During the First World War donkeys were sent from Lemnos in the Aegean Sea to Gallipoli in Turkey. These animals were put to work dragging ambulance wagons to and fro, hauling steel guns, water tanks, shovels and all manner of important equipment from barges on the coast to the trenches uphill and inland.

When they arrived off the coast of Gallipoli the donkeys were hoisted from the boat into the water and left to find their own way to dry land. Once on the beaches they were caught and tied up ready for work, except one who wandered in the wrong direction.

Private John Simpson Kirkpatrick loved donkeys. He had worked at a fair, running penny donkey rides for children when he was younger. He would ride one of the donkeys the two-mile journey home and treated them with such kindness and gentleness that they always responded well to him.

He was born in 1892 in South Shields, England. As a young man he joined the Merchant Navy but deserted ship when he was in Sydney, Australia. When war broke out in 1914 he enlisted in the Australian Imperial Forces and became one of Australia's national heroes.

He was sent to Gallipoli to serve in the Australian Army Medical Corps. Soon after he arrived, he found a forlorn looking donkey wandering around the rocky cliffs in the midst of gunfire and shell blasts. He befriended him and decided to call this donkey Murphy. He realised he would be a great help working with the wounded soldiers.

Private John Simpson Kirkpatrick and Murphy worked tirelessly over the following days. John would lay injured soldiers across Murphy's back and the donkey would take them to the medical tent. After only a few trips Murphy found the way on his own. When he reached the medical tents the staff would say to him, "back pedal", and he would back into the tent with his precious cargo of human life. Murphy and his new owner did this trip under heavy gunfire to Monash Valley and back to Anzac cove day and night. They saved the lives of more than 300 soldiers in conditions that were hazardous and life threatening, but they courageously battled on together.

On the 19th May 1915 John Simpson Kirkpatrick was shot dead by a machine gun. He was 22 years old and had been in Gallipoli for 24 days. Nobody knows what happened to Murphy after his owner's death.

Private John Simpson Kirkpatrick was twice recommended for the Victoria Cross and the Distinguished Conduct Medal, but he was never decorated for his actions.

Murphy was posthumously awarded the Purple Cross – the highest award available to animals – by the RSPCA. In South Shields a bronze statue of Private Simpson Kirkpatrick and Murphy commemorates their sacrifice.

Every year, on Anzac Day, the Australian newspapers run the story of Private Simpson Kirkpatrick and Murphy his donkey, their heroic contribution to the First World War never forgotten.

What happened to Murphy is a mystery. There were stories that he was adopted by an Indian Unit, but this could not be confirmed. After the publication of his story the Australian authorities searched for him, to evacuate him from the peninsula, but he could not be found.

Perhaps Murphy was returned to his home on Lemnos, and his descendants may be wandering the island to this day.